POSSESSING THE PROMISED LAND

Retreat Leader Guide

WORKBOOK

RICHARD T. CASE

Dedication / Acknowledgements

I wish to dedicate this course to and thank all of the leaders of our **Ministry: Living Waters—ABIDE Ministries!** along with my wife. Linda, who have all learned that:

1. God has promises for all of us personally
2. These promises are all "yes" in Him, and thus available to all and are true
3. These promises are potential and not guaranteed, as we have to walk with God to receiving these and have Him fulfill these for us.

As we have received and experienced these truths, we have together walked into these promises as God resolves our personal issues of life; and does not leave us to figure things out alone and thus live a life of frustration and resignation. Rather, we have learned to go to Him and ask Him what promise is He speaking to us, and then not to focus on the circumstances but continue to move forward with Him—knowing that He will fulfill what He speaks to us. The promise turns into reality for us. Our leader's experience this and then they give it away to their groups and friends who also learnt to hear, receive, believe and then experience God's promises for them. As the church universal grows in this, we will see a dramatic shift in the life of the church—from struggle and resignation to victory and joy. Thank you all for teaching these truths:

These leaders are:

Jake & Mary Beckel	Ed & Becky Kobel
Joe & Leigh Bogar	Don & Rachelle Light
Rich & Janet Cocchiaro	Chris and Heidi May
Larry & Sherry Collet	Terry & Josephine Noetzel
Scott & Kristen Cornell	Towanda Norton
David & Melissa Dunkel	Steve & Carolyn Van Ooteghem
Tom & Susanne Ewing	Preston & Lynda Pitts
Rick & Kelly Ferris	Dan & Kathy Rocconi
Joel & Christina Gunn	Bob & Keri Rockwell
Scott & Terry Hitchcock	John & Michelle Santaferraro
Rick & Nancy Hoover	Allyson & Denny Weinberg
Tad & Monica Jones	Neal & Kathy Weisenburger

Further, it is a joy for me to share this life with my wife, Linda, and family who especially continue to bring us back to seeking God's promises, stay in the process to receive these in our everyday lives and not go to discouragement and resignation. We get to enjoy the wonder and fullness of life because of living out this process.

POSSESSING THE PROMISED LAND
PUBLISHED LIVING WATERS—ABIDE MINISTRIES
7615 Lemon Gulch Way
Castle Rock, CO 80108

ISBN: 979-8-218-11538-8

Publisher's Cataloging-in-Publication data

Names:
Title:
Description: .
Identifiers: ISBN | LCCN
Subjects:

Printed in the United States of America 2024— 2nd ed

TABLE OF CONTENTS

Welcome to our course, Possessing the Promised Land. This is a wonderful opportunity for us to explore what God speaks about in terms of Christ's promises. There's a process of God speaking promises to us; and then we go to faith (believe it) and then possess it. This will show us that it is not just asking God to perform what we think He should do for us (typical prayer), but rather seeking, receiving, and experiencing His promises to us. We're going to go through the detail of this throughout this course.

Write out the promises that you have received from our Father (it matters not how long ago). What "Word" has He given you to confirm these promises? Which have been fulfilled? Which have not? What are your true thoughts in your heart about these promises for you personally? If you have not received any, or are not sure, this is not a problem as this is what we will learn.

Next, write out the difficult circumstances, issues, questions, decisions to be made, etc. for which you need God to reveal His will to you. This list will serve as context for what we learn in this course, and it will also be applied in your assignments.

LESSON 1:
THE REASONS FOR AND THE PRIVILEGE OF GOD GIVING EACH OF US PROMISES FOR THE SUPERABUNDANT LIFE

Write out what the following verses say about the nature and truths about God's promises. What is important to understand as we consider receiving God's promises?

> **Read 2 Corinthians 1:18–24:**
>
> [18] As surely as God is faithful, our word to you has not been Yes and No. [19] For the Son of God, Jesus Christ, whom we proclaimed among you, Silvanus and Timothy and I, was not Yes and No, but in him it is always Yes. [20] For all the promises of God find their Yes in him. That is why it is through him that we utter our Amen to God for his glory. [21] And it is God who establishes us with you in Christ, and has anointed us, [22] and who has also put his seal on us and given us his Spirit in our hearts as a guarantee.[d]
>
> [23] But I call God to witness against me—it was to spare you that I refrained from coming again to Corinth. [24] Not that we lord it over your faith, but we work with you for your joy, for you stand firm in your faith.

> "Faith is believing contrary to hope. The circumstances do not matter. He's spoken it."

The promises are not *yes* and *no*. If they were yes and no, what would they then become? Arbitrary. When I was a kid, I went to my mom and dad and asked if I could do this or that. Their response was usually *maybe*; which most likely meant what? No, probably not. It's arbitrary. But, the promises of God are not yes and no—rather, they are YES. And Amen. They're absolute. There are 7,000 of them in scripture. We start to realize all these as He speaks them to us, and He desires to speak to you. The key is that they're yes. Where? In Christ. So, as we look at promises, we don't have the right to simply name the promise and claim for our own…I want this one but not that one. We don't have the right to what's called "name it and claim it." Well, I want that one. So, I'm just going to take that one out of scripture as it applies to me. When we do this, we move to the flesh instead of being in the Spirit. If we are in the Spirit, they all are yes and according to His will. So, the key is being "in Christ." When in Christ, all of the promises are available to us. They are not arbitrary and are not just for lucky people (for some super spiritual). Rather, He says, "You're My child; they're all available to you. One hundred percent to everybody, all the time."

Our response is to be what? Yes. And Amen. Amen is not solely the end of a prayer. It also means, *It's done*. I've received what You had to say. I understand it applies to me. I believe it. May it now be so, so be it. I've gone through the process, and now I can say Amen. He said the promises that are all available are yes, and we are to complete it by coming to the Amen.

In what way was Abraham considered a great man of faith? What did he have to experience about understanding living out God's promises? What does this speak to how we are to grow in receiving His promises?

Read Romans 4:17–21:

[17] as it is written, "I have made you the father of many nations"—in the presence of the God in whom he believed, who gives life to the dead and calls into existence the things that do not exist. [18] In hope he believed against hope, that he should become the father of many nations, as he had been told, "So shall your offspring be." [19] He did not weaken in faith when he considered his own body, which was as good as dead (since he was about a hundred years old), or when he considered the barrenness[a] of Sarah's womb. [20] No unbelief made him waver concerning the promise of God, but he grew strong in his faith as he gave glory to God, [21] fully convinced that God was able to do what he had promised.

____

____

____

____

____

Faith is believing contrary to hope. The circumstances do not matter. He's spoken it. He says he believed it and the last statement, which is critical, Abraham was what? Fully persuaded, fully convinced that what God said, he would perform. God spoke it. And if He spoke it, it will happen. Where? In reality, in the real stuff of life. So, it's not about maybe and perhaps; it's the fact that He said it. So, we are persuaded. What does that imply?

There was a process of being convinced. As we look at Abraham's life, he was not considered a great man of faith. He tried to sell his wife twice. He tried to fulfill the promise himself by taking Hagar as his wife and then having Ishmael. He had a lot of failure. But because he stayed with the process, he became what? Fully persuaded that this was so and that he could trust it. We knew he trusted it when he was asked to sacrifice Isaac. He said, "The boy and I will come back." And in Hebrews 11:19, he believed that Isaac would be resurrected, which was interesting. At that point in time, there had been no resurrection, but that's what he thought. That's what was going to happen. He believed it. He'd been fully persuaded that God's promises are so and can't be thwarted when we are living in faith and have a heart to receive them.

Another example is the calling of the disciples. When Jesus invited them, His invitation was what? Come and see and follow Me. Were they great men of faith? No, they didn't have a clue what that even was. So, He starts to do miraculous things. And then He told the disciples to do them, too. But because they weren't sure they believed they'd be able to, they struggled a little bit with that. But what happened in three years? They were fully persuaded that they could believe what He spoke. It took three years. So, the encouragement to all of us is you're going to learn a lot of truth here. And your thought is going to be, I'm not there. He said, "That's all right. Do you have a heart to go because I'll persuade you. I don't mind persuading you," just as Abraham had been fully persuaded that what God said, he could perform.

What do these sets of verses reveal about His promises—what He speaks to us? On what basis is this true? What does this mean regarding our confidence in the promises? Why?

Read Ezekiel 12:25–28:

25 For I am the LORD; I will speak the word that I will speak, and it will be performed. It will no longer be delayed, but in your days, O rebellious house, I will speak the word and perform it, declares the LORD GOD."

26 And the word of the LORD came to me: 27 "Son of man, behold, they of the house of Israel say, 'The vision that he sees is for many days from now, and he prophesies of times far off.' 28 Therefore say to them, Thus says the LORD GOD: None of my words will be delayed any longer, but the word that I speak will be performed, declares the LORD GOD."

____

____

____

____

____

He's explaining that the words that He speaks will be performed. He reinforces that it is His spiritual power, which emanates from what He says that will accomplish what He will do in reality, in your circumstances, in the stuff that you're dealing with. So, it's not hypothetical. His power is superior, and He can fulfill what He speaks. This is not limited to natural solutions but the ability to speak things that do not exist and change circumstances.

Read Isaiah 55:8–11:

8 For my thoughts are not your thoughts,
   neither are your ways my ways, declares the Lord.
9 For as the heavens are higher than the earth,
   so are my ways higher than your ways

> and my thoughts than your thoughts.
> [10] "For as the rain and the snow come down from heaven
>   and do not return there but water the earth,
> making it bring forth and sprout,
>   giving seed to the sower and bread to the eater,
> [11] so shall my word be that goes out from my mouth;
>   it shall not return to me empty,
> but it shall accomplish that which I purpose,
>   and shall succeed in the thing for which I sent it.

____

____

____

____

____

He says: "My Word is going to succeed. It's going to fulfill what I say. I'm going to translate what I speak, My promise, into things that happen circumstantially. I'll make it happen. It will not return to Me empty. It'll accomplish its purpose." He started verse 8 saying, "My thoughts and My ways are not yours." So, as you're listening to the promise, what does that imply? Don't look for logical. Don't look for an answer logically in the natural. He says: "You have it all backwards. First of all, My ways and My thoughts are different than yours. I can do it in a different way. It's going to be supernatural, and how I do it will be unique to your situation."

For example, Joshua marching around Jericho. God told him to march around the city seven days and then blow his horn, and the walls will fall in, and they can go in and take the city. Joshua could have said, "I've got a great military plan. How about my plan?" God says His ways aren't our ways. How about if you just follow Him in faith and receive His promise. "Just march around and blow the trumpet. Because what I'm up to is going to be different than you planned." Joshua could have questioned Him by asking how that was going to work and when it was going to happen. (We'd like it done as soon as possible.) God says: "I'm not going to tell you either one of those. This is what possessing the promises is all about. You have to walk with Me into it in whatever way I choose. I'm likely going to do it in a way that you won't even understand so, there is no sense telling you. You just need to trust Me."

LESSON 1:
THE REASONS FOR AND THE PRIVILEGE OF GOD GIVING EACH OF US PROMISES FOR THE SUPERABUNDANT LIFE

In these sets of verses, what does God speak regarding who or what can annul (stop) the fulfillment of His promises, His Word? What then is critical to possessing the promises? Why is this so important to us, and therefore what must we consider to experience His promises?

Read Isaiah 14:24–27:

An Oracle Concerning Assyria
24 The LORD of hosts has sworn:
"As I have planned,
   so shall it be,
and as I have purposed,
   so shall it stand,
25 that I will break the Assyrian in my land,
   and on my mountains trample him underfoot;
and his yoke shall depart from them,
   and his burden from their shoulder."
26 This is the purpose that is purposed
   concerning the whole earth,
and this is the hand that is stretched out
   over all the nations.
27 For the LORD of hosts has purposed,
   and who will annul it?
His hand is stretched out,
   and who will turn it back?

He says, interestingly enough, all these potential obstacles are not a problem for Him. And He raises up a question: Who can annul it? What's the answer to that question? We can annul it. Nobody else. This is why the Promised Land and possessing is an act that we have to cooperate with because He said, "Here's where we're going, and it will be delivered here." The invitation is always, "Are you going to walk with Me and believe this? If you don't, if you're not willing to walk with Me and believe it, even though I'm giving you this promise, then you're the one who can annul it." It doesn't mean that He's not going to offer it to somebody else. It just means you're not going to participate in it. God's promises are always potential, but not guaranteed. We have to walk with Him. Many times, we say, "I think I believe this promise, or I see this promise, but I'm not willing to walk into it." And then we wonder, "Hey, I thought it was so." But God said, "Well, you stopped following Me."

Read Hebrews 3:15–19:

[15] As it is said,

"Today, if you hear his voice,
do not harden your hearts as in the rebellion."

[16] For who were those who heard and yet rebelled? Was it not all those who left Egypt led by Moses? [17] And with whom was he provoked for forty years? Was it not with those who sinned, whose bodies fell in the wilderness? [18] And to whom did he swear that they would not enter his rest, but to those who were disobedient? [19] So we see that they were unable to enter because of unbelief.

____

____

____

____

____

LESSON 1:
THE REASONS FOR AND THE PRIVILEGE OF GOD GIVING EACH OF US PROMISES FOR THE SUPERABUNDANT LIFE

This is the story of Moses and the Red Sea. They cross over miraculously, with the sea parting leaving dry ground for them to cross safely. Of course, as the Egyptians came, the sea returned to normal and flooded them, killing them all. But Moses and the Israelites are safe. They've crossed over and they're safe. What does God promise them? What does He say to them? That He'll take them to the Promised Land, the place of God fulfilling His promises to His children. Yes, there's an enemy there, but He'll defeat the enemy and deliver the land to them, a land of milk and honey abundance. And He'll give you great peace, and your life is going to be full of promises and all the things that He's ready to give you. They heard it, no issue.

What was their response? A little too scary. They're not going to do it. They don't believe it. If they are going do this, they're going to get killed. Our understanding from what we can see is we're going to get killed. And therefore, we're not going. It says in verse 19 that they could not enter the Promised Land because of their what? Unbelief. The word here, *unbelief*, is the refusal to be persuaded that what God had to say was true. They won't even consider it; they heard it, or they didn't even care to hear it, but they're refusing to be persuaded to believe that what God has to say is true. Also in verse 19, God said that as a result of their unbelief, what was the consequence? They wandered for 40 years, and they could not what? They couldn't receive the promise. He gave it to them and invited them to it. His expectation was that because He was speaking this to them personally (and My Word will perform what I speak), they'd say what? Amen, so be it. But instead, they said, "We heard it. We aren't going." He called them rebellious. And hard-hearted. And His attitude, His emotion toward them for 40 years was what? He was angry. He was not happy at all. Why was God angry? Because they wouldn't go with Him. They wouldn't possess the land with Him and listen and follow Him into it. They became stubborn. His heart was to give it to them, to fulfill His promise. His anger is about: "I have this beautiful thing for you. And you're refusing. You're refusing to process that with Me, and you are refusing to let Me give you the faith to believe it." It's absolute that He would. But still they refused. Two million people wandered around for 40 years, and never more than 11 miles from the Promised Land. The desert in Israel is awful. There are no trees. There's nothing to do. There are no cities. There are no games. There's nothing. There is just existing. He did take care of them by sending a cloud by day to protect them from boiling up and a fire by night to keep from the cold. He gave them manna, but still they were just existing. They're wandering around. So, what was God's will? To take them to the Promised Land of greatness, joy, abundance, peace. Did they experience God's will? No.

God didn't say, "I'm forcing you to do it, and I'm giving it to you anyway. It doesn't matter." It matters. What's your heart? Do you have a heart to go? Two million of them wandered around the rest of their life, never experiencing God's will, and they all died, not living in God's will. And there, by the way, was not a single new promise ever given to them. After that, they just wandered around. And that's also the state of the Christian Church; we're wandering around.

Most of us don't believe we can even hear a promise. Many others may believe but are still not sure about it. And since they're not sure, they aren't willing to go. So, God said, "My will is to give you these promises, and all the promises are what? Yes, and Amen. There are 7,000 of them, so, I've got an answer for you, and I will promise you this solution. Do you have a heart to hear, and then do you have a heart to receive it? The only one who can annul it, interestingly enough, is you, because it's about your heart."

What are the reasons that we typically give for not wanting to move forward into His promises? What is the difference between concerns and struggles and refusing to move forward because of the concerns and struggles? Why is this so important to our experiencing God's promises to us?

Read Numbers 13:25–4:4:

Report of the Spies

25 At the end of forty days they returned from spying out the land. 26 And they came to Moses and Aaron and to all the congregation of the people of Israel in the wilderness of Paran, at Kadesh. They brought back word to them and to all the congregation, and showed them the fruit of the land. 27 And they told him, "We came to the land to which you sent us. It flows with milk and honey, and this is its fruit. 28 However, the people who dwell in the land are strong, and the cities are fortified and very large. And besides, we saw the descendants of Anak there. 29 The Amalekites dwell in the land of the Negeb. The Hittites, the Jebusites, and the Amorites dwell in the hill country. And the Canaanites dwell by the sea, and along the Jordan."

30 But Caleb quieted the people before Moses and said, "Let us go up at once and occupy it, for we are well able to overcome it." 31 Then the men who had gone up with him said, "We are not able to go up against the people, for they are stronger than we are." 32 So they brought to the people of Israel a bad report of the land that they had spied out, saying, "The land, through which we have

> gone to spy it out, is a land that devours its inhabitants, and all the people that we saw in it are of great height. [33] And there we saw the Nephilim (the sons of Anak, who come from the Nephilim), and we seemed to ourselves like grasshoppers, and so we seemed to them."

____

____

____

____

They said, "Yes, the land is fantastic. But there's a giant enemy there, and they have never been defeated, so we'll probably get defeated." And they grumbled and complained. They don't like the place they're in. They have a problem and don't like it. But, remember, God had already told him what He was going to do. He was going to give them the Promised Land. Their response was that they didn't like it and then offered all of the excuses that we do as well.

1. "If only I had made a better decision back then, we wouldn't be in this pickle." We can look back and say, "Yes, maybe this problem is related to a decision I made before. If only I had done something differently. If only I had made a different choice, I would be in a different place and would not have to deal with this now. If only."

2. "Why has God brought us here to harm us. We are in this awful situation, and God's the one who brought us here." We're harmed because of God. Now think about that. What did God say? The opposite: "I'm taking you to the Promised Land." How did they flip from what God said was His promise to God's bringing us here to kill us? They were in circumstances they didn't think they could overcome on their own.

    One of the big things we hear all the time with Christians is, "Why didn't God take care of this? Why did God allow this to happen? Why? Why? Why? He says, "Do you have a heart to go to what I am going to deliver?" But, we flip it. He said they basically replaced truth with the lie. Why? Because they focused on the natural, focused on the circumstances.

3. "Wouldn't it be better if…?" In other words. I've got an alternative plan. Maybe it would be better if I come up with my own plan. I know better, and I trust my plan better than God's plan.

4. "I think I'll act on that plan. I am going to act in the natural and follow my own will."

5. That led them all to what? Never going to the Promised Land. They never said, "Well, let's follow God." Instead, they questioned why God brought them there if only to harm them. They, like so many, chose to solve their own problems, and thus rejected His promise. We reject Him and choose to go our own way. So, we then just wander around and die outside of His will, which is what they all did.

What do these sets of verses say was the difference in Joshua and Caleb that they were able to go to the Promised Land? What is required of us? Why? What does this mean for us personally? How might we then move forward to be willing to be like Joshua and Caleb and experience God's promises to us?

Read Numbers 14:24:

24 But my servant Caleb, because he has a different spirit and has followed me fully, I will bring into the land into which he went, and his descendants shall possess it.

God says: "Caleb and Joshua were able to go to the Promised Land." Why? Because they had a completely different heart. Do you have a heart to be persuaded that what God has to say is true? Do you want to go with God? Or are you deciding on your own? You're not going to receive the promise if you are not willing to go; but if you have a different heart and desire to go with Him, He will deliver to you the promise.

Read Hebrews 11:1–3:

By Faith

11 Now faith is the assurance of things hoped for, the conviction of things not seen. ² For by it the people of old received their commendation. ³ By faith we understand that the universe was created by the word of God, so that what is seen was not made out of things that are visible.

____

____

____

____

____

He sets up the whole understanding of why there's a promise. He said the world, the natural physical, the things that you have circumstantially, were created how? In verse 3, by the Word that God spoke. The material is subordinate to the spiritual. It's subordinate to what He says because His power is from His speaking. That's what He created everything with. He spoke it into existence. The material, your circumstances, are always subordinated to His promise. So that's why He says, over and over and over again: "Is anything too difficult for Me?" Why does He say that? Because He can speak to it and change it. His power is superior to that. In verse 1, He says it's the substance of things hoped for—the expectation that we are going to be delivered and the evidence of things not seen. Certainty of things not seen. It's not about what you observe or what you can figure out or come up with on your own. It's based upon certainty of what He says. You can be certain of that because it'll be so.

For example, if I said to you, "We're all going to the Rockies game tonight, and we're to meet at the entrance. We're all going to go in together with the tickets I got for you." I said it, but it hasn't happened yet. What would you do at six o'clock tonight? You go to the game. Why would you go to the game? Because the tickets are already done based upon what you were told. You're certain because I have credibility. You're certain it will be fulfilled. What you wouldn't do is call me every 10 minutes and ask, "Are you going? Are we going? Do you have the tickets? Are we really going to go? Are we really going to go? Are we really going to go?" This wouldn't happen because you're certain.

Secondly, you wouldn't talk yourself out of it. You wouldn't say, "I don't know. There's a lot of traffic. I'm not sure this electronic stuff's going to work. You know what? I don't think I should go. I'm not going," and you talk yourself out of it. Why? Because you're not certain. God said, "Faith is certainty," where you believe that what He says is true. That's the definition, which means we've got to get to that point. Do I have certainty about what He said? If He said it, I am certain it will happen. In verse 2, this happened with Joshua and Caleb. Moses and Aaron got a good report. What did Joshua and Caleb say? "Let's go! We agree with everything that those guys said about the difficulty of this situation. But God. And because God said, 'Let's go.'" We read in Numbers that when the other spies gave their report, it was called a bad report. What's the difference between a bad report and a good report? It's all based on the same facts. But what makes one good, and what makes one bad? What did God say? We're not disagreeing about the circumstance, but I've heard what God has to say about it, so I'll go with Him. That's called a good report. Or for a bad report, we understand the circumstances, we hear what God has said, but we are not going along with Him (i.e., a bad report). In other words, the circumstances are more important to me than what God said, even though I heard what God said.

As we are called to live by faith and believe the promises God made to us, what are the reasons that faith is required versus living by sight or by what is called, "Christian fatalism—whatever happens, happens?" What are the requirements to live by faith? What is the reward if we do meet the requirements?

Read Hebrews 11:6:

6 And without faith it is impossible to please him, for whoever would draw near to God must believe that he exists and that he rewards those who seek him.

It's impossible to please God without faith; to have faith, you must believe that He is. He can handle all. Nothing is too difficult for Him. You've got to believe He can handle your situation. If you've got an issue or you've got things that are problematic, He has something to say about that. Again, nothing is too difficult for Him. He said: "Diligently seek Me, and your role is to receive the reward. I'll give you the reward if you diligently seek Me. What's the reward of the promise? Fulfillment of the promise. But what's the reward that you're seeking? What do you need? Faith." Without faith, it is impossible to please Him. So, the thing you need is faith. God said, "If you diligently seek Him, He'll give you the faith," which is the exact thing you need. He will give it to you. In other words, who actually does that work? He does. It's not you working at having more faith. It's you saying, I have a heart to go and follow. You'll give it to me and then I'll understand it. I'll believe it, and I get to experience it.

LESSON 1:
THE REASONS FOR AND THE PRIVILEGE OF GOD GIVING EACH OF US PROMISES FOR THE SUPERABUNDANT LIFE

Read Hebrews 10:35–39:

[35] Therefore do not throw away your confidence, which has a great reward. [36] For you have need of endurance, so that when you have done the will of God you may receive what is promised. [37] For,

"Yet a little while,
    and the coming one will come and will not delay;
[38] but my righteous one shall live by faith,
    and if he shrinks back,
my soul has no pleasure in him."

[39] But we are not of those who shrink back and are destroyed, but of those who have faith and preserve their souls.

He says there is a reward for boldly walking with God and receiving His Word and then having the faith to believe it. After you have done His will (followed His steps of instruction to experience the promise, which is called walking into the promise), He will fulfill His promise. We must live by faith, not by sight, which He has no pleasure in. He said the key is to not throw away our opportunity to come to Him boldly where He will lead us into faith. He speaks, we process. He gives us faith to believe what He speaks so that we can experience the promise He has spoken.

LESSON 1:
THE REASONS FOR AND THE PRIVILEGE OF GOD GIVING EACH OF US PROMISES FOR THE SUPERABUNDANT LIFE

In these sets of verses, for us to receive the promises, how are we to specifically walk with God to possess them? How can we live this out in practical ways?

Read Deuteronomy 8:1–2; 6–10:

Remember the LORD Your God

8 "The whole commandment that I command you today you shall be careful to do, that you may live and multiply, and go in and possess the land that the Lord swore to give to your fathers. ² And you shall remember the whole way that the Lord your God has led you these forty years in the wilderness, that he might humble you, testing you to know what was in your heart, whether you would keep his commandments or not.

⁶ So you shall keep the commandments of the LORD your God by walking in his ways and by fearing him. ⁷ For the LORD your God is bringing you into a good land, a land of brooks of water, of fountains and springs, flowing out in the valleys and hills, ⁸ a land of wheat and barley, of vines and fig trees and pomegranates, a land of olive trees and honey, ⁹ a land in which you will eat bread without scarcity, in which you will lack nothing, a land whose stones are iron, and out of whose hills you can dig copper. ¹⁰ And you shall eat and be full, and you shall bless the LORD your God for the good land he has given you.

____

____

____

____

____

God speaks about how to receive His promises: "It's going to be fantastic if you go with Me, and it's going to be kind of barren and dry if you don't." And He said: "The key is to possess it. What is your role, your responsibility? Walk into it. Follow Me, I'm going to give you instruction. This time, this is the next generation." And He said, "Do you want to go?" They did. So, He offered them instructions—step by step. "If I were you, I'd follow the instructions because you will have to possess it.

What does that mean, possess? Own it. Enjoy it, receive it, live in it, experience it, make it yours, take hold of it. It is not hypothetical. It's real. I need you to possess it. If you're going to possess it, what does that imply about you? You have to be part of the process."

We have a tendency to think, "How nice that You gave me that promise. So, make it all happen. When You get it all done, let me know." Here the Israelites could have said, "OK, great, I'm glad You're taking us to this Promised Land. Defeat the enemy, make it all happen, and we'll just stay here on this side of the Jordan. And when You get it all done, let us know." God said: "No, you must possess it. You must own it. I'm calling you. The key is to follow My instruction. I will get you in the right place at the right time with the right people for Me to do My supernatural work of defeating the enemy. It's going to involve you possessing it, taking it on, and walking My way."

Read Deuteronomy 11:8–15, 18–25:

[8] "You shall therefore keep the whole commandment that I command you today, that you may be strong, and go in and take possession of the land that you are going over to possess, [9] and that you may live long in the land that the LORD swore to your fathers to give to them and to their offspring, a land flowing with milk and honey. [10] For the land that you are entering to take possession of it is not like the land of Egypt, from which you have come, where you sowed your seed and irrigated it,[a] like a garden of vegetables. [11] But the land that you are going over to possess is a land of hills and valleys, which drinks water by the rain from heaven, [12] a land that the LORD your God cares for. The eyes of the LORD your God are always upon it, from the beginning of the year to the end of the year.

[13] "And if you will indeed obey my commandments that I command you today, to love the LORD your God, and to serve him with all your heart and with all your soul, [14] he[b] will give the rain for your land in its season, the early rain and the later rain, that you may gather in your grain and your wine and your oil. [15] And he will give grass in your fields for your livestock, and you shall eat and be full.

[18] "You shall therefore lay up these words of mine in your heart and in your soul, and you shall bind them as a sign on your hand, and they shall be as frontlets between your eyes. [19] You shall teach them to your children, talking of them

when you are sitting in your house, and when you are walking by the way, and when you lie down, and when you rise. [20] You shall write them on the doorposts of your house and on your gates, [21] that your days and the days of your children may be multiplied in the land that the LORD swore to your fathers to give them, as long as the heavens are above the earth. [22] For if you will be careful to do all this commandment that I command you to do, loving the LORD your God, walking in all his ways, and holding fast to him, [23] then the LORD will drive out all these nations before you, and you will dispossess nations greater and mightier than you. [24] Every place on which the sole of your foot treads shall be yours. Your territory shall be from the wilderness to[a] the Lebanon and from the River, the river Euphrates, to the western sea. [25] No one shall be able to stand against you. The LORD your God will lay the fear of you and the dread of you on all the land that you shall tread, as he promised you.

____

____

____

____

____

God says, "Follow My instruction, follow Me, cling to Me. Love Me, have a heart to go where I'm taking you. I'll give you the power to follow it. So, stay with Me. Stay with Me. Stay with Me. That's how you're going to possess it, because I'm going to give you step by step instructions." As a result of your affection for Him, you will surrender to Him saying, yes, you want to follow Him. Yes, you want to hear what He has to say because His way is best and none better. His will is going to give you His promise to you. He will fulfill you. This promise is going to be spectacular, and you'll just go with Him as He does His work in the process.

God shows us the difference between living in the flesh, the natural, in a difficult and troubled world, and living in the Spirit, the supernatural in the power of the Kingdom. There's Egypt with the mediocrity and difficulty (oppression). The burden to maneuver through this place is on those who have decided to live in the flesh, but there is also the opportunity for living in the Promised Land, which is spectacular. Who's going to take care of it? He said: "I'll take care of it. You've been burdened and have struggled. My promise is better. I'm going to give you this fantastic place, and I'll take care of everything. I'll have you possess it and then deliver to you the beauty of that. This is an absolute wonderful truth—you don't have to like what you have been doing on your own, or be responsible to take care of your own things any longer.

If we do learn to walk with Him, what is His promised result for us? What does that mean for our personal lives? Why will that then encourage us to learn this even further?

> **Read Deuteronomy 5:31–33:**
>
> 31 But you, stand here by me, and I will tell you the whole commandment and the statutes and the rules that you shall teach them, that they may do them in the land that I am giving them to possess.' 32 You shall be careful therefore to do as the LORD your God has commanded you. You shall not turn aside to the right hand or to the left. 33 You shall walk in all the way that the LORD your God has commanded you, that you may live, and that it may go well with you, and that you may live long in the land that you shall possess.

____

____

____

____

____

He keeps reiterating: "It's going to go well. It's better if you follow Me. I can deliver things that you can't." He says, as we walk with Him, He will reveal whether we should turn to the right or to the left. What does that imply? That He will tell you which way to go. We don't have to decide based on some natural or logical analysis. He will lead.

But, why would you follow His instruction? Why do you trust Him? What do you believe about Him? He knows more than we do. He knows what's around the corner. Have you ever been in a corn maze in the fall? You get in. You're in the middle of it. And what do you do? Go down the path. Dead end. Come back. Dead end. You're going different directions trying to find your way, but it's not working well. God says: "I am standing up on the tower. I see the entire thing. And when we are at a fork, a crossroads, I will tell you which way to go." Why? Because He sees the whole thing. He knows the right path, and thus we find our way easily. His heart is to reveal this path to us—His best and none better.

He says: "If you're going to walk with Me, you're going to hear My instruction now, which is turn right or turn left." What does that imply? It's specific. It's not a generic, "Good luck, I hope you make it. I hope you find your way out of the maze." Rather, He knows the path, and His directions will be specific.

What choice does God give us regarding how to experience His promises? What does it mean, and how do we live this out? What are the real elements of the choice to be made?

Read Deuteronomy 30:11–20:

The Choice of Life and Death

[11] "For this commandment that I command you today is not too hard for you, neither is it far off. [12] It is not in heaven, that you should say, 'Who will ascend to heaven for us and bring it to us, that we may hear it and do it?' [13] Neither is it beyond the sea, that you should say, 'Who will go over the sea for us and bring it to us, that we may hear it and do it?' [14] But the word is very near you. It is in your mouth and in your heart, so that you can do it.

[15] "See, I have set before you today life and good, death and evil. 16 If you obey the commandments of the LORD your God[a] that I command you today, by loving the LORD your God, by walking in his ways, and by keeping his commandments and his statutes and his rules,[b] then you shall live and multiply, and the LORD your God will bless you in the land that you are entering to take possession of it. [17] But if your heart turns away, and you will not hear, but are drawn away to worship other gods and serve them, [18] I declare to you today, that you shall surely perish. You shall not live long in the land that you are going over the Jordan to enter and possess. [19] I call heaven and earth to witness against you today, that I have set before you life and death, blessing and curse. Therefore, choose life, that you and your offspring may live, [20] loving the LORD your God, obeying his voice and holding fast to him, for he is your life and length of days, that you may dwell in the land that the LORD swore to your fathers, to Abraham, to Isaac, and to Jacob, to give them."

He said: "This isn't that difficult. You don't need somebody else to get it for you. You don't need to be sophisticated to get it. You don't need somebody to go a distance to get it. It's in My mouth. I speak; now, you receive it and speak it. It'll be clear." He said, "To walk with Me is based upon the fact that I set before you life or death, blessing or cursing. I'm going to give you the choice." The choice that He defines in verse 20 is to walk with Him. That's your choice. It's not you figuring out what is the right way. See the difference? He says, "I'll tell you that your choice, if you're going to choose life and blessing, is to walk with Me, cling to Me." Then He gives a little hint. "Hear My voice. I'll speak it to you." Instruction. That's what walking with Him looks like. We are understanding, hearing, following. It will be clear to us. His role is to make it clear.

Then, He gives an interesting statement in verse 17, "The way to walk with Me is hear My voice; and when you don't hear Me anymore, it's an issue that your heart has turned away." Now, think about the simplicity of that in light of what He just said, "I've set before you life or death, blessing or curse cursing. If I were you, I'd choose life. But when your heart turns away, what have you chosen? Death. Because what did you decide? To do it your own way. Choosing not to walk with Him. And when you do that, He said: "You've stopped hearing My voice. It's a pretty good indicator if you are choosing Me or not; are you hearing Me or not. And if you are not hearing Me, because you've walked away from Me, I have a remedy for that…just come on back."

It says you can make the choice now. Let's go. I know you went to the wrong place. I know you went down the wrong path at the crossroad, and you weren't supposed to be there. What can God do? He can recalculate. Like a GPS, when you receive instructions from the GPS, but you think you know better, and you keep going. Finally, what does the GPS do? Recalculates. It doesn't matter how far you have gone astray, God is going to give you a new route. Do you have a heart to follow that? That's the beauty of God. He doesn't ask for perfection, but instead a heart to go, to follow Him. And He says, when you stop hearing, you've walked away, and you probably went down some paths you weren't supposed to. But He can take care of it. How about now? Let's go.

Noting the questions or issues we wrote originally, what is God speaking to us? What instructions is He giving? How are we to walk with Him specifically to possess these?

____

____

____

____

____

____

____

____

LESSON 2:
HOW WE RECEIVE AND EXPERIENCE IN REALITY THESE PROMISES FOR US PERSONALLY

Possessing the Promised Land is about our walk with God as He leads us into His fulfillment of His plan for us: Plans for good, and plans for a beautiful future. This is the Covenant. He is going to bless you to make you a blessing. This involves Him speaking promises. We have issues, we have decisions, we have adversity. What have you heard, or what are you wanting to hear about? He'll speak to that precisely, and He'll speak His promise to us personally. All the promises are yes in Christ, which means we have to receive it from Him. We can't just decide on our own. As we've learned, it's potential but not guaranteed—we have to have a heart to walk with Him into the promise and possess it, own it, take hold of it. So now, we'll go deeper into this aspect of walking with God. What does it mean to walk with God? What is our role?

As we learn to walk with God into His promises for us, how do we apply taking down, eliminating idols in our lives? For us, what are some of those idols, and why are they considered idols for us? What is the benefit of us removing them from our lives?

Read 2 Chronicles 17:1–6:

Jehoshaphat Reigns in Judah

17 Jehoshaphat his son reigned in his place and strengthened himself against Israel. ² He placed forces in all the fortified cities of Judah and set garrisons in the land of Judah, and in the cities of Ephraim that Asa his father had captured. ³ The Lord was with Jehoshaphat, because he walked in the earlier ways of his father David. He did not seek the Baals, ⁴ but sought the God of his father and walked in his commandments, and not according to the practices of Israel. ⁵ Therefore the Lord established the kingdom in his hand. And all Judah brought tribute to Jehoshaphat, and he had great riches and honor. ⁶ His heart was courageous in the ways of the Lord. And furthermore, he took the high places and the Asherim out of Judah.

____

____

____

____

____

Jehoshaphat walked with God and followed Him—following the instruction of God—with a heart to follow God. We decide, "I'll stay with Him. I'll obey His voice." As a result, God specifically said not to put anything else above Him, which in essence are idols. So, if you're going to walk with Him, it is important to review your life and identify anything that is more important than Him. Jehoshaphat did and took down the idols that were in the way of his and Israel's relationship with God. He put God preeminent, making sure that nothing was in the way. We need to evaluate anything in our life that is ahead of God or draws us away from walking with God. This includes: I've got a system. I've got a person who I trust more than God. I have work that I trust more than God. Those things have to come down and be replaced with putting God preeminent, first, in all of life.

From these sets of verses, what is the importance of abiding? How do we define abiding? What is the reason that God invites us to abide in order to receive His promises? If we do abide, what result will we experience? What does that mean in our everyday lives?

Read John 15:1–5:

I Am the True Vine

15 "I am the true vine, and my Father is the vinedresser. [2] Every branch in me that does not bear fruit he takes away, and every branch that does bear fruit he prunes, that it may bear more fruit. [3] Already you are clean because of the word that I have spoken to you. [4] Abide in me, and I in you. As the branch cannot bear fruit by itself, unless it abides in the vine, neither can you, unless you abide in me. [5] I am the vine; you are the branches. Whoever abides in me and I in him, he it is that bears much fruit, for apart from me you can do nothing.

He defines what it means to walk with Him—abide in the vine and let the vine dresser make your decisions, give you instruction, give you the promises. What does that mean to abide? To stay in the relationship, to stay connected to receive His life, His promises. The promises are conditional upon us abiding in Him. Apart from Him, we can do nothing. You won't receive promises if you are apart from Him. It won't be fulfilled because you won't hear it, and you won't possess it. So, abiding is critical.

He says: "By the way, enjoy the walk because you'll bear much fruit. You're going to receive these promises that I am delivering to you, which will lead to a grand, covenant life.

Read John 8:28–32:

28 So Jesus said to them, "When you have lifted up the Son of Man, then you will know that I am he, and that I do nothing on my own authority, but speak just as the Father taught me. 29 And he who sent me is with me. He has not left me alone, for I always do the things that are pleasing to him." 30 As he was saying these things, many believed in him.

The Truth Will Set You Free
31 So Jesus said to the Jews who had believed him, If you abide in my word, you are truly my disciples, 32 and you will know the truth, and the truth will set you free."

Christ states, "The way that I function with the Father is I only do what pleases Him. Whatever He spoke or He promised, I followed. He gave instruction. I saw the supernatural. I experienced it. I exercised it, I possessed it. I only did what the Father led Me to. You can do the same thing. If you abide, remain, stay with My word to you, then what happens? I speak to you. You will know the truth, and the truth will make you free—set you free. You'll enjoy freedom. You'll enjoy beauty. Go where I'm speaking and let Me speak to you through My word of the promises that I'm going to give you, and then abide there. If you stay there until you receive faith, you're going to experience My promise. And then, go possess it step by step by step. The question is really simple: Do you believe it?" If you say yes, what's coming next? A test? God will say, "Let's go find out." Things aren't going to work out according to plan now. He's going to see if you believe it. If you don't believe it, He's inviting you to stay with Him longer. He will always have more to give you. You think you have it on your own? You don't.

The second thing to ask is, "Are you experiencing it?" Knowing about it doesn't mean experiencing it. If you haven't fully abided yet, then He hasn't released you yet, because He's going to carry you all the way through. Most Christians think God will just give them information. You go to Bible studies. You read. You think you know a lot about it. But are you experiencing it? Well, no. Well, then, what good is it to know about it? Stay with it. Stay with it. Stay with it. Because He said, He'll give it to you, and you will be set free. Experience the joy in the freedom of what He's going to give you. If you abide in His Word, you know the truth to set you free.

Even if you believe God can deliver promises, what is still necessary for us to experience them? What is the difference between rejecting this and receiving this? How do we then practically live this way?

Read Psalm 86:8–13:

[8] There is none like you among the gods, O Lord,
   nor are there any works like yours.
[9] All the nations you have made shall come
   and worship before you, O Lord,
   and shall glorify your name.
[10] For you are great and do wondrous things;
   you alone are God.
[11] Teach me your way, O Lord,

> that I may walk in your truth;
>
> unite my heart to fear your name.
>
> [12] I give thanks to you, O Lord my God, with my whole heart,
>
> and I will glorify your name forever.
>
> [13] For great is your steadfast love toward me;
>
> you have delivered my soul from the depths of Sheol.

His promises are true. But what are we asking Him to do? Teach us to walk in His way. This implies we have a heart to go. What's now required? That we give it time and energy, because we have to learn it. We need Him to teach us to walk in His way. If He's teaching, our role is to be a receiver. And teaching, by the way, implies what? To demonstrate by receiving His instruction and correction. He is saying, "Did you know that I spoke, and you didn't listen and instead walked away? Come on back. Hey, did you realize that you heard my voice and it really worked, and you got that exciting thing? Do you appreciate that? Do you see the difference? Do you understand what it is?" God is teaching you through the Holy Spirit.

Next, he says, "Unite my heart with you. Make me so that I have a motivation, a desire, the same thing that You see, I see and put my heart in that place, unite me with the Spirit that I walk in unity with. I'm praying for that. I'd like to experience that. I'd like to have the unity of understanding that what You say is true: the fear of the Lord. I believe it now. Unite me to walk into that place where it is in my heart level, not perfunctory."

Why would you have a heart to do it? Because His way is best, and none better. And, we want the best. So therefore, we are going with Him. It's really that simple. And of course, the starting point is to admit, "I'm not so sure about that because I haven't experienced that. God understands that I am struggling with conflict, deep problems, messes, and they said God was in control. How come, how come, how come this is happening to me? Maybe there is something I don't understand." Would you be willing to learn how to walk with Him? He'll give you the Covenant, bless you to make you a blessing, and He'll restore this issue you have now. We don't know how or when. If you have a business problem, for example, we don't know His answer to the problem. He actually might take you through bankruptcy because he's got something on the other side of it. We may not know His specific answer for you, but we do know the truth and can guarantee He will resolve, restore, and deliver to you the Covenant life. It's always the best, and it's always fun, and it's always filled with surprises. Does that mean you won't have any trouble? No, but since He's already taken care of it—already disarmed principalities, powers, and rulers, we don't have to worry about that part of it. We have to surrender to His way of bringing it about and walk with Him.

What are the consequences of not walking with Him? For God to deliver His promises, what is He waiting for? What are we then to wait for? How does the Spirit guide us along His path to the promises? How does this practically work for us?

Read Isaiah 30:15–26:

[15] For thus said the Lord God, the Holy One of Israel,
"In returning[a] and rest you shall be saved;
   in quietness and in trust shall be your strength."
But you were unwilling, [16] and you said,
"No! We will flee upon horses";
   therefore you shall flee away;
and, "We will ride upon swift steeds";
   therefore your pursuers shall be swift.
[17] A thousand shall flee at the threat of one;
   at the threat of five you shall flee,
till you are left
   like a flagstaff on the top of a mountain,
   like a signal on a hill.
The Lord Will Be Gracious
[18] Therefore the Lord waits to be gracious to you,
   and therefore he exalts himself to show mercy to you.
For the Lord is a God of justice;
   blessed are all those who wait for him.

[19] For a people shall dwell in Zion, in Jerusalem; you shall weep no more. He will surely be gracious to you at the sound of your cry. As soon as he hears it, he answers you. [20] And though the Lord give you the bread of adversity and

> the water of affliction, yet your Teacher will not hide himself anymore, but your eyes shall see your Teacher. [21] And your ears shall hear a word behind you, saying, "This is the way, walk in it," when you turn to the right or when you turn to the left. [22] Then you will defile your carved idols overlaid with silver and your gold-plated metal images. You will scatter them as unclean things. You will say to them, "Be gone!"
>
> [23] And he will give rain for the seed with which you sow the ground, and bread, the produce of the ground, which will be rich and plenteous. In that day your livestock will graze in large pastures, [24] and the oxen and the donkeys that work the ground will eat seasoned fodder, which has been winnowed with shovel and fork. [25] And on every lofty mountain and every high hill there will be brooks running with water, in the day of the great slaughter, when the towers fall. [26] Moreover, the light of the moon will be as the light of the sun, and the light of the sun will be sevenfold, as the light of seven days, in the day when the Lord binds up the brokenness of his people, and heals the wounds inflicted by his blow.

He says, "If you follow Me, it's going to go well for you, but you tend not to."

You say, "Well, I know better."

He says, "When you say you know better, what happens? It doesn't go well."

You say, "I know better. I'm not sure that God's will is best and none better."

He says, "Well, how's it going? How's that working out for you so far? Why don't you try something different? I'm waiting for you."

What is He waiting for? For us to stop trying to figure this out on our own. He's waiting for us to have a heart to follow Him—to receive His mercy. The words here are "Covenant loyalty." He's going to deliver the Covenant to you.

He's waiting for you to say, "OK, let's go." In verse 18, He asks that you wait for Him to hear what He has to say and then take the time to understand it, walk into it, and possess it. He's not going to run ahead of you. He wants you to wait for His instructions step by step by step. He says that if you do that, your teacher, the Holy Spirit, will never be shoved off into the corner, but instead will bring the directions—turn left or right—that you seek. The Spirit will reveal the path. The Spirit will tell you what to do. You'll hear a voice from behind you speaking. He purposely says it this way. Why? Because we tend to look only at what's in front of us. We see it, we observe it. We figure things out by our sight. But He says that we'd be better served if we didn't focus on what we see, but instead listened to what God was saying. If I took you blindfolded and walked you to your car, what would you have to rely on? What I say. Take the next step. Step down, stop, turn right, turn left. I'll get you there. And you can't rely on your sight at all. You would have to listen to me and trust me. I know where we're going. I'm going to get you there. And that's why He says the voice comes from behind you. You're not focusing on what you see. You're focusing on what you hear. He'll give you the answers: the promises, truth, direction, and instruction. And then it's going to go well for you.

For what must we wait? Why? What is the benefit of waiting? Why is this attractive for us and motivate us to wait versus move ahead on our own?

Read Isaiah 40:31:

31 but they who wait for the LORD shall renew their strength;
   they shall mount up with wings like eagles;
they shall run and not be weary;
   they shall walk and not faint.

____

____

____

____

____

While you expect an answer, you're willing to wait until you get the answer, and then receiving the clarity and the understanding that goes with it. Instead of wanting it right now (our typical approach), He says we are better off waiting to receive it along His path (step by step), and in His timing. We are to enjoy the wait because we get to have fellowship together, we get to have unity together.

Then He said, "What happens when you wait?" You live with the freedom and perspective of wings like eagles and you run and not grow weary and you walk and you don't faint. He's giving you the picture of an eagle. What does an eagle do? He soars above it all and sees it all. You get to see what God sees. You get to see the bigger story. You get to see things that He's up to. And it's freedom. It's soaring. It's beautiful. It's mighty and majestic. That's where He wants to take you if you wait. That's what you will experience, and you'll be strengthened; you won't faint and you won't be weary because by definition, His path for you is pleasant. His path for you is margin. His path for you is joy and shalom, because in the Kingdom of God is righteousness, peace, and joy. Wait.

As we experience His promises, what is the true purpose of this? In what way do we express this purpose? Why is this so important to possessing the Promised Land?

Read Isaiah 42:5–9:

5 Thus says God, the LORD,
   who created the heavens and stretched them out,
   who spread out the earth and what comes from it,
who gives breath to the people on it
   and spirit to those who walk in it:
6 "I am the LORD; I have called you[a] in righteousness;
   I will take you by the hand and keep you;
I will give you as a covenant for the people,
   a light for the nations,
7   to open the eyes that are blind,
to bring out the prisoners from the dungeon,
   from the prison those who sit in darkness.
8 I am the LORD; that is my name;
   my glory I give to no other,
   nor my praise to carved idols.
9 Behold, the former things have come to pass,

> and new things I now declare;
> before they spring forth
> I tell you of them."

He says, "This path is for whose glory? My glory, not yours." You get to participate in it, you get to experience it. But it's going to glorify Him, which by definition, if it's going to glorify Him on our path, He must intervene and do the supernatural, not the natural. We thus cannot say, "I could have done that." Instead, you look at what God did, which is the path that He wants us to go on. It's His promise to you that if you walk on His path, you're going to be part of it. You are going to become the Covenant yourself. What does that mean? He has promised blessings for you, and then He's going to ask you to give it away. It's actually going to come through you. You are the Covenant. So, the bigger story of why God wants you to walk with Him and His promises and possess the promises is so that you can be the Covenant to others, which is a great honor and privilege. This is how He describes our role in the Covenant: Open the blind eye and bring them out of prison (bondage to the flesh, and their natural patterns that contribute to sadness, unhappiness, and oppression/burden). This includes people who don't understand what you're talking about. But we can help. We want to be the Covenant. Now, we can't do that unless we're experiencing promises, so we can help others understand what it looks like. Then your eyes will be opened, and you'll come out of prison, and you'll get to experience it, too. And by the way, we know something about your path. If you start receiving this, walking into His promises and living out this path, walking with Him, we know what is going to happen to you. You will also become the Covenant. It's absolute. And, as you do that for others, guess what? They will become the Covenant. And on and on and on. So, the offspring and the fruit are beyond what you'll ever imagine. You know you're going to become the Covenant and be part of God's bigger story.

From these sets of verses, what are the elements of walking with God, and how do these apply practically to us? Why are they so important? Why are all three needed?

> **Read Ephesians 5:1–2:**
>
> *Walk in Love*
> **5** Therefore be imitators of God, as beloved children. [2] And walk in love, as Christ loved us and gave himself up for us, a fragrant offering and sacrifice to God.

____

____

____

____

He said that as you're walking with Him, you are to walk in the love, the affection of Christ, who was the fragrant offering of life for us. When you love somebody, what is your heart toward them? Your heart wants to serve them. You look after them. You want to be with them. So, He says, "Walk in the fact that I have affection for you. I want to be with you. I want you to enjoy Me. I love you. I want to protect you, and I want to take care of you. Walk into My love. Walk with My love."

> **Read Ephesians 5:8–11:**
>
> [8] for at one time you were darkness, but now you are light in the Lord. Walk as children of light [9] (for the fruit of light is found in all that is good and right and true), [10] and try to discern what is pleasing to the Lord. [11] Take no part in the unfruitful works of darkness, but instead expose them.

____

____

____

____

____

Walk in the light. He says, "As you walk in the light, you're going to be led into truth. So, as you're walking, you're always open to the light and the truth. I would like you to know the truth and be receiving and willing to receive the truth about all and every one of the issues/questions/decisions in your life." You are to receive the truth, which is the light. God says, "Let me show you the light. I know more than you." When we sense something's not right, or realize that we do not have God's answer, the question is really simple. What's the truth? Lead us to that. Now that you have a heart to go, let's go. Remember, sometimes it's about you. Maybe there is something that God wants to heal, transform, build in our life so he can build His character in us. Always be willing to go because He wants you to stay in the light. He says, "Discover what's acceptable to Me—My will." Go find God's will, which is going to be discovered in the truth. Trust the truth. And you stand on the truth.

Read Ephesians 5:15–21:

[15] Look carefully then how you walk, not as unwise but as wise, [16] making the best use of the time, because the days are evil. [17] Therefore do not be foolish, but understand what the will of the Lord is. [18] And do not get drunk with wine, for that is debauchery, but be filled with the Spirit, [19] addressing one another in psalms and hymns and spiritual songs, singing and making melody to the Lord with your heart, [20] giving thanks always and for everything to God the Father in the name of our Lord Jesus Christ, [21] submitting to one another out of reverence for Christ.

Walk in wisdom. You're seeking answers from who? God. Why? He knows more than you do. He knows the way. He knows the best, and He can deliver the best. As we walk in wisdom, we expect and have settled that He will give you the wisdom. And He says, "What you're looking for is to discover My will. I'll reveal My will through My wisdom. Walk in that. The key is not to grieve the Holy Spirit. How would you? The word *grief* means being sad, which makes sad the Holy Spirit." How could you make sad the Holy Spirit? Ignore what He said. Or do not care about even hearing what He says. Decide you are going your own way, that you are not willing to walk with God. He said, "That saddens Me. Why? Because I love you. I've got this fantastic thing for you. I want to heal you, I want to lead you to the very best—the Covenant—and you're not willing to receive My wisdom. I don't get that. It makes Me sad. You're preventing Me from doing it. I have a heart to do it, but you're not willing to stay with Me to receive it." Speak to each other with psalms and hymns—the Word of God—keep reminding each other of that and then submit to one another. What are you submitting to? Unity with the Spirit. Let's go together and let the Spirit give us wisdom. And submit to that. Let's go to God. If we disagree with someone in our life, it's okay. We know that eventually we'll get the answer because the same Holy Spirit in you is the same Spirit in me, right? And He cannot tell the two of us two different things. So, we're agreeing to submit to following Him, walking with Him. He describes it by walking in love, walking in the light, walking in wisdom. How? Together. Do that together.

That's what it means to walk with Him. He said, "I'll deliver the promise." We know that we have an enemy. And if God wants to give us the promise, what's the enemy's goal? Steal it from you.

How does this set of verses describe the work of Satan? What is his purpose? What are his strategies toward this purpose? How do we fall into his strategies (to what does he appeal, and why do we fall for it)? What is the result when we do?

Read John 10:10:

10 The thief comes only to steal and kill and destroy. I came that they may have life and have it abundantly.

____

____

____

____

____

> **Read Ephesians 6:10–13:**
>
> The Whole Armor of God
> [10] Finally, be strong in the Lord and in the strength of his might. [11] Put on the whole armor of God, that you may be able to stand against the schemes of the devil. [12] For we do not wrestle against flesh and blood, but against the rulers, against the authorities, against the cosmic powers over this present darkness, against the spiritual forces of evil in the heavenly places. [13] Therefore take up the whole armor of God, that you may be able to withstand in the evil day, and having done all, to stand firm.

____

____

____

____

____

God speaks here of the schemes of the enemy who is working against you through his wiles, and strategies. Remember Satan isn't God, but he's a finite angel with lots of demonic helpers. They're observing you constantly. If you're walking in love, walking in the light, walking in wisdom, the promise will be fulfilled. So, what then is the enemy's goal?

To get you out of walking with God—in love, in the light, in wisdom. "Don't walk there. Walk over here where I have you, and I can steal from you because I understand something. God's promises are potential, not guaranteed." What's required for it to be fulfilled? You have to possess it. How do you possess it? Walk with Him. That's clear. That's known. It's known by the enemy. Therefore, his goal is to get you to what? Stop walking. Stop walking and God will not deliver you the promise. He understands that. And that's why we are not to live in the thinking that whatever happens, happens. We are not to be Christian fatalists. So, the scheme is to cause you to get to the flesh and to stop walking with Him. Rather, walk on your own; and, when you're walking on your own, who's got more power over you? Satan. He has you. And he's just thwarted God's will. He's just thwarted the fulfillment of the promise, which is why a lot of Christians are experiencing a lot of difficulty, because they're not living in that process and the enemy's got them walking in a different way. He has an interesting technique that started way back with Adam and Eve.

Read Genesis 3:1–5:

The Fall

3 Now the serpent was more crafty than any other beast of the field that the Lord God had made.

He said to the woman, "Did God actually say, 'You[a] shall not eat of any tree in the garden'?" 2 And the woman said to the serpent, "We may eat of the fruit of the trees in the garden, 3 but God said, 'You shall not eat of the fruit of the tree that is in the midst of the garden, neither shall you touch it, lest you die.'" 4 But the serpent said to the woman, "You will not surely die. 5 For God knows that when you eat of it your eyes will be opened, and you will be like God, knowing good and evil."

____

____

____

____

____

So, you are in the process of promise. What were Adam and Eve told by God about the tree in the center of the garden? Do not eat of it, because if you do, you will surely die; and I'm giving you authority over the whole place. Go tend it, take care of it. My promise is that you are going to have this beautiful place expanded throughout the world, under you and your offspring. That's my promise. And by the way. You can eat of everything. You can go wherever you wish. However, don't do what? Don't eat of that tree, which is a test of the will – whom will you love, trust, and serve? Satan comes along. And first of all, he says, what? Surely, what did God really say? They were a little bit unclear about that. And this is why they were there many, many years. It wasn't just 10 minutes in a little patch in the back, and they fell and it was over. So, when we're receiving our promise and walking into a promise, the enemy tempts us to consider: Did God really say it, and is it starting to cause doubt? We need to think, "Did I really hear right? Maybe He didn't say that promise to me. Maybe that was me. What did God really say?" Then think: Yes, I heard it, but it is not going to be fulfilled. And you partly buy into it because why? It hasn't happened yet. So, what do you do? You go do your own plan. You think you'll fulfill it.

We have a perfect example of Abraham and Sarah. God gave them a promise but it wasn't happening. What did they decide to do? They called upon Hagar. You do as Hagar did and have Ishmael. Isn't that it how we shall experience the promise? We will help God fulfill it. Is it really going to happen? Well, maybe not. Did God stop Abraham and Sarah from doing that? No, His will is clear to you. His promise is clear to you. The mistake they made at that moment was that they didn't go back to God and say, "We have this great idea to fulfill Your promise (which isn't happening on our time)." Then they implement their "good" idea. Even though this was not God's will, He did not stop them. His will and promises are by invitation and not by force or interfering with free will. After they had Ishmael, God said to them: "Now that you have Ishmael, that's not the answer." Abraham says, "Why don't you just use him. We already have him. Why don't you just use him?" But he is not the promise, and as matter of fact, you have to cast him out because he's not the promise. "Do you have a heart to go now and receive My promise, which still is an invitation to you, even with your mistake of the flesh?" To Abraham's credit, he said, "OK, sorry, I made a mistake. Cast him out. I'll believe you." And then he had Isaac which led to the fullness of the promise.

The enemy's schemes are to create doubt and have you stop walking with God by walking your own way. But because nothing is currently happening, you wonder if is it really going to happen? The enemy is constantly whacking you. Did God really say it is going to happen? Maybe not. Maybe you didn't hear Him right, etc. The enemy is trying to thwart you from possessing it. This is all termed "temptation."

Read James 1:12–18:

[12] Blessed is the man who remains steadfast under trial, for when he has stood the test he will receive the crown of life, which God has promised to those who love him. [13] Let no one say when he is tempted, "I am being tempted by God," for God cannot be tempted with evil, and he himself tempts no one. [14] But each person is tempted when he is lured and enticed by his own desire. [15] Then desire when it has conceived gives birth to sin, and sin when it is fully grown brings forth death.

[16] Do not be deceived, my beloved brothers. [17] Every good gift and every perfect gift is from above, coming down from the Father of lights, with whom there is no variation or shadow due to change.[a] [18] Of his own will he brought us forth by the word of truth, that we should be a kind of firstfruits of his creatures.

Every good gift is from God—through speaking promises and then making it happen: "I can deliver it, and it's going to be spectacular, over the top, amazing. Every amazing thing that I have planned for you is My will. My promises will be delivered and are coming from Me. However, the enemy is trying to get you away and keep you away from that." This is what God calls sin, and sin leads to death. What does that mean? Death of the spiritual process and power of the life of the Spirit in delivering the promise to you in your real life. The promise that you've been given is now dead. Sin leads to the promise going to death. The promise now cannot happen. So, the enemy is trying to get you to sin.

Ok, let's back up another step. How does he do that? By appealing to your desires—to self-determination and pursuit of your own way—walking on your own path. If you do this, if you fall for this, you act on what you think you know better—my great idea. What are you actually doing? You put to death the promise. Because you didn't stay with it and because you're not possessing it.

Let's look at examples in scripture of how the enemy works.

First, what is the promise given to Nehemiah, and how did he receive it. Was he then willing to walk into it?

Read Nehemiah 1:1–11:

Report from Jerusalem
1 The words of Nehemiah the son of Hacaliah.

Now it happened in the month of Chislev, in the twentieth year, as I was in Susa the citadel, [2] that Hanani, one of my brothers, came with certain men from Judah. And I asked them concerning the Jews who escaped, who had survived the exile, and concerning Jerusalem. [3] And they said to me, "The remnant there in the province who had survived the exile is in great trouble and shame. The wall of Jerusalem is broken down, and its gates are destroyed by fire."

Nehemiah's Prayer
[4] As soon as I heard these words I sat down and wept and mourned for days, and I continued fasting and praying before the God of heaven. [5] And I said, "O Lord God of heaven, the great and awesome God who keeps covenant and steadfast love with those who love him and keep his commandments, [6] let your ear be attentive and your eyes open, to hear the prayer of your servant that I now pray before you day and night for the people of Israel your servants, confessing the sins of the people of Israel, which we have sinned against you. Even I and my father's house have sinned. [7] We have acted very corruptly against you and have not kept the commandments, the statutes, and the rules that you commanded your servant Moses. [8] Remember the word that you commanded your servant Moses, saying, 'If you are unfaithful, I will scatter you among the peoples, [9] but if you return to me and keep my commandments and do them, though your outcasts are in the uttermost parts of heaven, from there I will gather them and bring them to the place that I have chosen, to make my name dwell there.' [10] They are your servants and your people, whom you have redeemed by your great power and by your strong hand. [11] O Lord, let your ear be attentive to the prayer of your servant, and to the prayer of your servants who delight to fear your name, and give success to your servant today, and grant him mercy in the sight of this man."

Now I was cupbearer to the king.

Nehemiah was part of the remnant that Jeremiah had prophesied to the nation of Israel. If you repent because you're all doing your own thing and you're not following God, you're going to get judged and Nebuchadnezzar is going to come and capture you.

And God tells Jeremiah, "You know what? Stop telling them to repent. It's going to happen. So now appeal to the remnant and say to them, 'If you have a heart to follow Me, I'll still deliver the Covenant even though you're going to get captured.'" Fortunately, many of them did follow this instruction. Part of that life was Daniel and Meshack, Shadrach, and Abednego. They have the example of them living this grand life in the remnant. Now it's about one hundred years later, and Nehemiah is a Jewish student of the Word, taught to follow God, taught to have a heart for God, and he's never been in Israel. And God gives him an instruction, gives him a promise: Build the wall. "I'm going to send you back, and you're going to rebuild Israel, and we're going to reestablish the nation of Israel. You're the guy." And then he prayed for four months to process. Really? Me? And God says, "Let me confirm it. Let me verify it. Let me help you understand it. I will include specific details. You're going to need provision, but just ask the king and he will give it to you. He's been praying for four months to understand and confirm the promise—My assignment, My detailed instruction, My work through Nehemiah. There is a time for this to come about, today is the day. Get ready to ask the king. You're going to start the possession of this promise today. Let's go."

The king blesses Nehemiah, and he goes to Jerusalem. There he does an evaluation of the wall and tells everybody, "God's going to restore us; join His work of rebuilding as God has promised us." Then, the enemy works his schemes:

From these sets of verses, what were the strategies of the enemy, and how did Nehemiah respond?

> **Read Nehemiah 2:10:**
>
> 10 But when Sanballat the Horonite and Tobiah the Ammonite servant heard this, it displeased them greatly that someone had come to seek the welfare of the people of Israel.

____

____

____

____

When Satan and the demonic see that you're starting the possession of the promise, what's their perspective? They're unhappy. They're going after you. In other words, they're coming after you now. This is not going to be a cakewalk because the enemy is present and going to work to thwart you experiencing God's will. It is Satan coming after you. And you're the recipient of it.

> **Read Nehemiah 2:19:**
>
> 19 But when Sanballat the Horonite and Tobiah the Ammonite servant and Geshem the Arab heard of it, they jeered at us and despised us and said, "What is this thing that you are doing? Are you rebelling against the king?"

____

____

____

____

____

The enemy is coming against you to convince you that you're doing the wrong thing. They jeer, cast negative thoughts, negative ideas, convince you that it is not what you think it is going to be, that you're doing something wrong.

Read Nehemiah 4:1–3:

Opposition to the Work

4 [a] Now when Sanballat heard that we were building the wall, he was angry and greatly enraged, and he jeered at the Jews. [2] And he said in the presence of his brothers and of the army of Samaria, "What are these feeble Jews doing? Will they restore it for themselves?[b] Will they sacrifice? Will they finish up in a day? Will they revive the stones out of the heaps of rubbish, and burned ones at that?" [3] Tobiah the Ammonite was beside him, and he said, "Yes, what they are building—if a fox goes up on it he will break down their stone wall!"

____

____

____

____

____

The technique is: This isn't going to work. This will never work. You'll never fulfill this, and it'll never happen. It's easy to buy into it because at the moment, it isn't happening and you're seeing that things aren't coming together. Remember, God said, He is still going to fulfill it. Do you believe it? Don't let the enemy convince you that this is never going to happen—especially when you are going down a path with God that you have not experienced before. Nehemiah had never been to Jerusalem before. He's never built a wall in a place of utter ruin with people who have been living an oppressed life. This is a risky thing. This is a new thing. This is a new path and God says, "I'm going to deliver it to you, but you're going to have to trust Me." And the enemy is trying to say, "Don't trust it. It'll never work."

Read Nehemiah 6:1–14:

Conspiracy Against Nehemiah

6 Now when Sanballat and Tobiah and Geshem the Arab and the rest of our enemies heard that I had built the wall and that there was no breach left in it (although up to that time I had not set up the doors in the gates), ²Sanballat and Geshem sent to me, saying, "Come and let us meet together at Hakkephirim in the plain of Ono." But they intended to do me harm. ³And I sent messengers to them, saying, "I am doing a great work and I cannot come down. Why should the work stop while I leave it and come down to you?" ⁴ And they sent to me four times in this way, and I answered them in the same manner. ⁵ In the same way Sanballat for the fifth time sent his servant to me with an open letter in his hand. ⁶ In it was written, "It is reported among the nations, and Geshem[a] also says it, that you and the Jews intend to rebel; that is why you are building the wall. And according to these reports you wish to become their king. ⁷ And you have also set up prophets to proclaim concerning you in Jerusalem, 'There is a king in Judah.' And now the king will hear of these reports. So now come and let us take counsel together." ⁸ Then I sent to him, saying, "No such things as you say have been done, for you are inventing them out of your own mind." ⁹ For they all wanted to frighten us, thinking, "Their hands will drop from the work, and it will not be done." But now, O God,[b] strengthen my hands.

¹⁰ Now when I went into the house of Shemaiah the son of Delaiah, son of Mehetabel, who was confined to his home, he said, "Let us meet together in the house of God, within the temple. Let us close the doors of the temple, for they are coming to kill you. They are coming to kill you by night." ¹¹ But I said, "Should such a man as I run away? And what man such as I could go into the temple and live?[c] I will not go in." ¹² And I understood and saw that God had not sent him, but he had pronounced the prophecy against me because Tobiah and Sanballat had hired him. ¹³ For this purpose he was hired, that I should be afraid and act in this way and sin, and so they could give me a bad name in order to taunt me. ¹⁴ Remember Tobiah and Sanballat, O my God, according to these things that they did, and also the prophetess Noadiah and the rest of the prophets who wanted to make me afraid.

____

____

____

____

____

Think about what the enemy is doing and doing relentlessly: Don't try this. I'm coming against you. I'm using the anger of someone in the family (a fellow Jew) who said, I prophesied that this is going to happen. Come and be with me in the temple. They're going to try to kill you. You need to go hide. Stop your walk of possessing the promise. Do something different that will meet your personal desire. You know what you're doing is wrong. This is awful.

Then he proceeds to make lies against him. Satan is trying to bring you to his game to come over to his side. Nehemiah understood this, and said, "I'm not even going to bother with you guys because I'm not going to play your game. I know what you're up to."

As you read through the whole story of Nehemiah, God gave him step by step instructions. He was working to deliver the promise and gave him the courage to fight against the enemy.

What are we experiencing in our walk that we now see are strategies of the enemy to distract us, to thwart the promises of God? How might we respond as Nehemiah did? What shall we then expect? Why?

____

____

____

____

____

____

____

As we conclude this lesson, we understand that God says: "Walk with Me, and I'm going to deliver the promise. As you go to possess it, I'll give you instruction. I'll tell you to turn right, turn left. I know more than you. I can see the whole thing. Come and let Me deliver it to you. Stay with Me, walk in the light, walk in love, walk in wisdom." We understand that the enemy is going to try to thwart you from receiving the promise, to get you away from walking with God and back into the flesh. He'll try to get you to come on his turf where he can thwart God's will because God isn't going to fulfill it when you're not walking with Him.

We are called to make a choice—even though you may be struggling with it because you're getting distracted, perhaps discouraged, we need to understand that the enemy is trying to thwart it—so choose not to fall to temptation, but rather stay with God through faith and courage to possess the promise.

LESSON 3:
THE ROLE OF PRAYER AND BEING LED BY THE SPIRIT IN RECEIVING THESE PROMISES FOR US PERSONALLY

As we now are in Lesson 3 of Possessing the Promised Land, let's summarize what we have learned so far: God gives promises, and all the promises are yes in Christ. He says, "My heart for you and My path for you, My life for you is what I'm going to do for you. And what I am going to do for you is based upon My promises that I'm going to fulfill, which I will speak to you. So, possessing these promises requires faith—certainty of things not seen—and what we can be certain of is what He speaks. He said, "Your role is to hear what I have to say and then possess it. Go in step by step by step, follow My instruction, and be in the right place at the right time with the right people so that I can fulfill My promises." That's His way of life for us, which is magnificent. The Covenant. He's going to bless you to make you a blessing.

We also know we have an enemy who wants to thwart us from receiving God's magnificent life for us. He needs to get us out of that Kingdom to a place of the self. And we described his technique and his wiles: He's watching us and trying to entice us to think that God's plan isn't going to happen. We should go and just develop our own plan. As we get into Lesson 3, we're going to look at how to overcome that and live the beautiful life of God.

From this set of verses, in order to stop the activity of the enemy who is working to thwart the possessing of the promises of God, what are we called to do? What does that look like? What is the result?

> **"He said, "Your role is to hear what I have to say and then possess it."**

Read James 4:7–10:

7 Submit yourselves therefore to God. Resist the devil, and he will flee from you. 8 Draw near to God, and he will draw near to you. Cleanse your hands, you sinners, and purify your hearts, you double-minded. 9 Be wretched and mourn and weep. Let your laughter be turned to mourning and your joy to gloom. 10 Humble yourselves before the Lord, and he will exalt you.

____

____

____

____

____

We resist this technique of the devil by submitting ourselves to God. Submitting ourselves to God means we are willing to believe that what He says is true. Remember, His promises are potential but not guaranteed. Why? He must be King of His Kingdom, and thus we are called to surrender and say we'll go with You, to have You give me the faith to believe it so that You can fulfill it. Think of the Israelites who had escaped Egypt, crossed the Red Sea, and were given the promise of God delivering them the magnificent life in the new land, but they could not enter the land of promises because why? Unbelief. Unbelief is the "refusal to be persuaded that what God had to say was true." The enemy will try to get you away from that. God says to resist the wiles of the enemy, which can be completely counteracted by continuing to surrender to God, keep following God, keep letting Him guide and lead you. Then absolutely the devil has to flee. This is really simple. How come the devil must flee? The supernatural trumps the natural. All the time, every time. And when we're abiding, living in the supernatural, we have power over the natural.

By submitting to God, where are you living? With the King, in the heavenly, in His Kingdom where the supernatural operates. Satan has to flee because you've gone to this place of safety that he can't touch. So, he has to flee; he has to stop his activity. Even though we may have to process having a little bit of doubt (I wonder if this is really going to happen), we go right back to God. "God, what do you have to say about this? I'm struggling, but could You help me understand? Could you clarify and reinforce that You are going to fulfill what You just said, and then I'll going to surrender to You and live in Your Kingdom?" Then the enemy stops his activity because we've surrendered and humbled ourselves to God. We tend to think of humble as lowly to the point of having nothing or being nothing. That's not humility. In scripture, it said that the most humble man of history was Moses. Was he nothing? No. The definition of humility is this: You seek God's will over yours. And why would that be humble? I get myself out of the way and come into agreement with God's will, and His promises come to me. That's humility. I believe God. I seek God's will over mine. Why? His way is best and none better. If you really understood that, would you stay in that place of humility? Sure. All the time. Ask God: Would You help me? Would You give me strength? Would You give me reinforcement? I'm going to seek You. Give me the faith to believe the promise that You've given me. The enemy then stops the attack, flees and I continue then to walk into the promise without the wiles of the enemy.

> **Read 1 Peter 5:5–11:**
>
> 5 Likewise, you who are younger, be subject to the elders. Clothe yourselves, all of you, with humility toward one another, for "God opposes the proud but gives grace to the humble."
>
> 6 Humble yourselves, therefore, under the mighty hand of God so that at the proper time he may exalt you, 7 casting all your anxieties on him, because he cares for you. 8 Be sober-minded; be watchful. Your adversary the devil prowls around like a roaring lion, seeking someone to devour. 9 Resist him, firm in your faith, knowing that the same kinds of suffering are being experienced by your brotherhood throughout the world. 10 And after you have suffered a little while, the God of all grace, who has called you to his eternal glory in Christ, will himself restore, confirm, strengthen, and establish you. 11 To him be the dominion forever and ever. Amen.

____

____

____

____

____

God will fulfill the promise. Believe that God will fulfill the promise. Don't worry about this issue. He's going to resolve it. Believe it. Go back to humility. Seek God's will over yours. As you strengthen in your faith, remember He's the finisher of faith. He's the one who gives you faith. So, the simplicity is that you're going to be strengthened by faith. Where do you have to be? In heaven, with Him, who's going to give you the faith. Just keep coming back. And He says, "Cast all your cares upon Me."

If you're in the middle of the struggle, issues of life decisions, things aren't working out too well and you're seeking God, ask Him, "God, what do You have to say about this?"

As He again reiterates His promises to you, the enemy is trying to cast doubt on that. We are to cast our cares upon Him. We do not focus on all the potential negative outcomes, or the wiles of the enemy who is working to cast doubt on this ever happening. No, cast that all onto God and let Him replace our cares with His promise and His fulfillment of His promise. Look again at the example of the Israelites: The 10 spies said the outcome is going to be bad, because we're going to get killed. What did Joshua and Caleb say? "But, God said, 'see the difference?' It is okay for me to understand the difficult circumstances we are facing. But, God said: 'Let's go follow that.'" How? By casting our cares onto Him and letting Him guide us to the victory of experiencing His promises.

We are called to bring down strongholds. How are these defined? What impact do they have toward us enjoying life? How do we bring them down? How does this practically work in our daily lives?

Read 2 Corinthians 10:1–6:

Paul Defends His Ministry
10 I, Paul, myself entreat you, by the meekness and gentleness of Christ—I who am humble when face to face with you, but bold toward you when I am away!— ² I beg of you that when I am present I may not have to show boldness with such confidence as I count on showing against some who suspect us of walking according to the flesh. ³ For though we walk in the flesh, we are not waging war according to the flesh. ⁴ For the weapons of our warfare are not of the flesh but have divine power to destroy strongholds. ⁵ We destroy arguments and every lofty opinion raised against the knowledge of God, and take every thought captive to obey Christ, ⁶ being ready to punish every disobedience, when your obedience is complete.

____

____

____

____

____

He says, "Cast down the strongholds of the way you're thinking." Take every thought captive to who? Christ. Remember, we talked about walking in the light as one of the aspects of walking with God. Well, one of those elements is that the light is based on the truth. This is why we help each other. What do you thinking about, where are your thoughts going? The enemy is trying to persuade us that the outcome is going to be bad, and so wants us to focus on the circumstance, and take things into our own strength—our own plan—the flesh. That's what you're thinking is. When you think that, what do you do? You speak about it. "Woe is me. This isn't going to work, oh my, I don't think God's going to do anything." You start talking as if it is not going to happen. Paul says we are to take every thought captive to whom? Christ. Based on the light of it (the truth). We are to help each other take our thoughts captive to Christ: I hear you speaking this. What are you thinking about? I'm thinking about this awful thing that could happen. Okay, why don't we go back to God and cast that down and let Him replace that with His Word? The promise? Let's get back to the promise. Let's get back to the Word of God. That's why it's so critical that faith comes from hearing, and hearing from the Word. Let's get back to that. I know the giants are there. Yep, I understand that. Yes, I see the possibility of that. When you are in the middle of the struggle, it's really difficult to switch our thinking. That's why we need each other. "I'm not denying that truth, but why don't we go back to God and focus on what He has spoken (pulling down strongholds and taking our thoughts captive to His truth)."

What did Joshua and Caleb do? Even though the circumstances were negative, they said, "But, God. I believe Him—what He promised, let's go." Their minds were on God while the other ones were on the circumstance—and they weren't willing to take every thought captive. And because of that, God said they could not enter the Promised Land. Where your mind goes will dictate your ability to receive faith; you could stay in that negative and never get there because you refuse to take your thoughts captive to Him. One of the issues we face is that, not only are you thinking negatively, but you're also laying on guilt that you can't do it, which is a double stronghold. That's why you need each other. Go back to God. Cast down every stronghold and take your thoughts captive to Him.

First, how did Peter receive revelation, the promise of God? Why was this so significant, and how then do we receive revelation and promises?

> **Read Matthew 16:13–20:**
>
> *Peter Confesses Jesus as the Christ*
> [13] Now when Jesus came into the district of Caesarea Philippi, he asked his disciples, "Who do people say that the Son of Man is?" [14] And they said, "Some say John the Baptist, others say Elijah, and others Jeremiah or one of the prophets." [15] He said to them, "But who do you say that I am?" [16] Simon Peter replied, "You are the Christ, the Son of the living God." [17] And Jesus answered him, "Blessed are you, Simon Bar-Jonah! For flesh and blood has not revealed this to you, but my Father who is in heaven. [18] And I tell you, you are Peter, and on this rock[a] I will build my church, and the gates of hell[b] shall not prevail against it. [19] I will give you the keys of the kingdom of heaven, and whatever you bind on earth shall be bound in heaven, and whatever you loose on earth shall be loosed[c] in heaven." [20] Then he strictly charged the disciples to tell no one that he was the Christ.

____

____

____

____

____

This is where Jesus says to His disciples, "Who does everybody say I am?" Elijah. John the Baptist. Jeremiah. And, He said, "Well, who do you say I am?" And Peter says, "You're the son of the Living God, the Messiah." And Jesus said, "Well done. The Father has given you this revelation. You've received it by faith. You get it. Hallelujah. Upon this ability to receive faith, I'm going to build My church. You have the power to bind and loose, and I'm going to build My church on this truth, which is the promise. You received truth. You believed it. And now you can move forward."

What is the reason we tend not to walk with God but actually are following the schemes of the enemy? What mistakes do we tend to make, just as Peter did? Why is this so significant to learning to walk with God? What then is the process to be able to walk with God (follow Him)? What does this mean personally to how we live this out?

Read Matthew 16:21–23:

Jesus Foretells His Death and Resurrection

21 From that time Jesus began to show his disciples that he must go to Jerusalem and suffer many things from the elders and chief priests and scribes, and be killed, and on the third day be raised. 22 And Peter took him aside and began to rebuke him, saying, "Far be it from you, Lord![a] This shall never happen to you." 23 But he turned and said to Peter, "Get behind me, Satan! You are a hindrance[b] to me. For you are not setting your mind on the things of God, but on the things of man."

Peter had just said, "You're the Messiah." And Jesus responded, "You know, well done. You received this from God. By the way, I'm going to go to My death and I'll be resurrected." Peter's response to that was what? I am not going to let that happen. And if we were to ask Peter, "Do you think you just said something good," what would he say? "Of course. I am not going to let Him go to death. I'm not doing that." And Jesus' response? "Get behind Me, Satan." Thirty minutes before this, Peter was the most spiritual person there was. But, in 30 minutes, he went to living the life of Satan. Get behind me, Satan. Jesus says, "You do not have your mind on the things of God but on the things of men—the flesh, your great idea. You have lost what's on the heart of God, and instead went with that you thought was a good idea." What's the mistake that Jesus said Peter made? "You didn't keep listening and processing and receiving what I had just said. I spoke something. If you're going to follow God, it's not that you have to immediately understand it—rather, when you do not quite understand it, go to God to help you understand what was spoken." Jesus would have explained all this to Peter, but Peter skipped seeking the things of God. He didn't ask for an explanation.

He reacted with, "I'm not listening to what you said. I'm going to go do what I think is best," which is the flesh. It is then that you're moving into the world and under the influence of Satan.

> **Read Matthew 16:24–28:**
>
> Take Up Your Cross and Follow Jesus
> 24 Then Jesus told his disciples, "If anyone would come after me, let him deny himself and take up his cross and follow me. 25 For whoever would save his life[a] will lose it, but whoever loses his life for my sake will find it. 26 For what will it profit a man if he gains the whole world and forfeits his soul? Or what shall a man give in return for his soul? 27 For the Son of Man is going to come with his angels in the glory of his Father, and then he will repay each person according to what he has done. 28 Truly, I say to you, there are some standing here who will not taste death until they see the Son of Man coming in his kingdom."

He says, "If you're going to live a life of faith and receiving My promises, deny self. Surrender with humility, My will to yours. I stand on the cross." Satan's been defeated and He's given us the victory of power; I join Him in overcoming; and then I'm going to follow Him. Follow Him where? Into the promise. He's going to speak: "This is what I'm going to do. Walk with Me here, let's go possess it." You will have real issues, circumstances, negative stuff that has and will happen to you. Yes, you're part of the world. God says, "I'll speak to every one of them, constantly. If you deny yourself, take up the cross and follow Me, I will resolve all and every one of these. Follow Me by walking with Me. I am on a path. It's not an event. We're going to have milestones because I'm going to fulfill things." But guess what? That just leads to the next part of the path, which also will require faith, as without faith it is impossible to please Him.

In order for us to follow Him (after denying self, and standing on the truth of the cross), what is required? What exactly is this, and in what way can we be certain which is the requirement? Then, how do we receive faith? What is the role and responsibility of Jesus in this process? Why is that important for us to understand and not take on His responsibility?

> **Read Hebrews 11:1–3:**
>
> By Faith
> **11** Now faith is the assurance of things hoped for, the conviction of things not seen. ² For by it the people of old received their commendation. ³ By faith we understand that the universe was created by the word of God, so that what is seen was not made out of things that are visible.

____

____

____

____

____

Faith is the certainty of things not seen, but certain in what He speaks to us—He explains why. The world was created by what He spoke. It's called Ex-Nihilo—creation out of nothing. He spoke it into existence; it was all created by Him through Him and for Him—by speaking—not forming or shaping what was already there. No, speaking it into existence out of nothing. The spiritual, the supernatural, the Word is superior to the material. You've got a circumstance, you've got adversity, you've got a problem, you've got a decision to make. You have issues. God says, "Is anything too difficult for me? Why not? Because I'll speak to it. I can change it. My power is superior to any circumstance you've got. I can speak to this. And, by the way, in addition to that, I'm going to give you wisdom to get in the right spot for Me to fulfill My promise to you. While you're walking with Me, I want you to have joy. Don't worry about this circumstance. Cast your care upon Me. I'll give you a resolution, and I can do it supernaturally by speaking to you. I want your heart to enjoy the walk, and I want you to see that I'll fulfill what I say by speaking it. And you can be certain of that."

LESSON 3:
THE ROLE OF PRAYER AND BEING LED BY THE SPIRIT IN RECEIVING THESE PROMISES FOR US PERSONALLY

Read Hebrews 12:1–2:

Jesus, Founder and Perfecter of Our Faith

12 Therefore, since we are surrounded by so great a cloud of witnesses, let us also lay aside every weight, and sin which clings so closely, and let us run with endurance the race that is set before us, ² looking to Jesus, the founder and perfecter of our faith, who for the joy that was set before him endured the cross, despising the shame, and is seated at the right hand of the throne of God.

____

____

____

____

____

Christ is the author and founder of faith and the perfecter and finisher of faith. He is both. How does He author faith? He speaks it, and that's why when you have a circumstance, which we all are going to have, you say to each other, with your small group, as a couple, as a family, a simple question: What do You have to say about this? What are You going to speak about this situation? What wisdom do You have to reveal to me? How do I follow you? What's Your promise? Instead of me figuring it out, He will show me the way. He'll author it by saying, "My Word to you is this…" Get confirmation and go to unity. Did I hear it right? Do I understand it? Do I have clarity about that? That's where you have to spend your time. It's not, "I'm not sure about this, how does this apply to this? Am I receiving it right?" (We'll talk about how you get confirmation.) But once you have confirmation, you say, "OK, I heard what you had to say, now, who's responsible for getting it to certainty? He is. It is not, "I heard it. I'm going to work at getting faith." If you approach it this way (your responsibility to get faith, you actually walk backwards and you can't get it, because you're in the flesh, not in the Kingdom. We have to let Him finish it: "Let Me finish it. I'll finish it." And that's why He says, "I'll test it." James 1:2–8 says: I'm going to test it. You think you have it but you fail the test and you really don't. What does that imply? Keep with it. Because He, in Romans 10:17, says that faith comes from hearing, hearing from the Word of God. So, your focus is on the Word—what He's spoken and your role is hearing it, receiving it, processing because that's where faith will come. When you take your thoughts captive and you processing together, it goes back to the Word. Get your mind back on the Word. Abide there, because that's where faith comes. What did God say? Keep going because He'll perfect it. And He said, "Do you have the things of man on your mind? In other words, are you stuck with what you and others are trying to figure out on your own, as opposed to what I have to say? Believe what I have to say. Stay with Me until I finish it, which is certainty." Move to: You know that you know that you know.

As we then move to faith, what is important in the process, and what truths do we reach in the process? (How do we know we have faith?) When we know that we know that we know, how then are we to pray? Why?

> **Read 2 Samuel 7:25–29:**
>
> 25 And now, O LORD God, confirm forever the word that you have spoken concerning your servant and concerning his house, and do as you have spoken. 26 And your name will be magnified forever, saying, 'The LORD of hosts is God over Israel,' and the house of your servant David will be established before you. 27 For you, O Lord of hosts, the God of Israel, have made this revelation to your servant, saying, 'I will build you a house.' Therefore your servant has found courage to pray this prayer to you. 28 And now, O Lord GOD, you are God, and your words are true, and you have promised this good thing to your servant. 29 Now therefore may it please you to bless the house of your servant, so that it may continue forever before you. For you, O Lord GOD, have spoken, and with your blessing shall the house of your servant be blessed forever."

____

____

____

____

The context here is David had, toward the end of his life, been taking to different places, what's called the Tabernacle, the tent of meeting where they would worship God in a tent. And it was being moved around from place to place to place. And David says, "You know, I really think it's a good idea that we make a permanent place, the temple. Let's build God a temple. I'm going to build the temple for God, and I'll do this for God. Isn't this a good idea?" He goes to Nathan, the prophet, seeking confirmation. And Nathan said, "Yeah, that's a good idea. Yep. Go ahead." In the same chapter, God goes to Nathan and said, "Come here. You guys forgot something, you never asked Me." And Nathan says, "Whoops. Sorry. You're right. Yep, sorry. Forgot to ask You." If you go back to what happened with Peter, what would God say to them? "Get behind me, Satan. You guys just decided on your own what you thought was a good idea." Is it a good idea? Yes. Was it God's idea? No. If it's not God's idea. He's calls it what? Evil. We must clearly see the difference—is it of the flesh or is it of the Spirit.

God says, "David is not building Me a temple. He's a man of war. He is not building me a temple, but his son can. Actually, I have a promise for David. Tell David that out of his lineage is going to come the Messiah," which, by the way, was the first time it was ever specifically spoken. We knew back in Genesis that God had spoken that the Messiah was going to crush the head of Satan—but now He is speaking that the Messiah will come through David. "Go tell David that's My promise to him." David then says, "I heard what you said, and I found courage in my heart to pray it." This is really the key to it: What did he pray? What does it mean he found courage in his heart? He prayed and prayed and prayed and found courage in his heart to take the energy to understand and receive this promise (receive faith).

In verse 28, "Now I know; I have certainty now. I have clarity. You are God, You're my guide, and I'm not God. You can deliver this promise. I receive Your words. Your words and what You speak is true. I absolutely believe that Your words are absolutely true. They're not a maybe. They're true. You have promised this to me, and I receive, understand, and have clarity that this promise is particularly applicable to me. I acknowledge You as God. You can do this. What You've said, I acknowledge, is true. The Messiah is coming through me, and this is applied to me. This promise is to me personally. The prayer of courage is getting to understand what you've said, this applies to me, and it's true.

In verse 29, he says, "Amen. May it please You to fulfill what You say." The prayer shifts. He spent all of his time getting to understand what He said, and realize it applied to him. Once that's true, this is a certainty of faith. Once you have that, what now does your prayer say? Therefore, may it please you to fulfill it. It shifts. It's not, "Did I hear correctly? Are you going to do it? I wonder if it's going to happen." You have this settled, you stop asking for that. Now, do it, fulfill it, so be it. "Amen. I now expect it and am excited to see you fulfill it."

From this set of verses, what is the process of how we understand His will, receive His will, and then experience His will (His promises to us)? What demonstrates that we are following the process and can be assured we will experience possessing the promises?

> **Read 1 John 5:14–15:**
>
> ¹⁴ And this is the confidence that we have toward him, that if we ask anything according to his will he hears us. ¹⁵ And if we know that he hears us in whatever we ask, we know that we have the requests that we have asked of him.

____

____

____

____

____

This too is simple. God says, "Your role is to pray, according to My what? To My will, you pray according to My will." This is a significant statement. If you're going to pray, according to His will, what must He do? Tell you His will. He must speak His will. And I must be able to hear it and receive it so I can pray according to His will. He says, "When you pray back to Me, I'm listening. What is He verifying? What is He listening for? That you heard this and understood this. Did you understand His will? If you don't understand His will, what is He going to do if you have a heart to receive it? He will say, "Let Me clarify it for you. Let Me give you clarity. Let Me help you understand it. I want you to know this is very specific. It's applied to you in this circumstance. And when you pray it, you know that I've heard it, it's going to happen." Why is it going to happen, even though we may be waiting for its fulfillment? He spoke it. Why did He speak it? Because His will is best and none better. "I speak it, you receive it, and when I know you have received it and believe it, I will perform what I spoke (My will). And, I can deliver this regardless of circumstances, because I can. My Word, My power is super to the natural." The only thing that is going to stop it is us. Why? If we do not have a heart to receive His will by not taking the time or the energy to come to clarity about it, He then lets us wander around—even for the rest of our lives. Go ahead. He says, "If I were you, I'd choose to follow My will—it is far superior to your will."

LESSON 3:
THE ROLE OF PRAYER AND BEING LED BY THE SPIRIT IN RECEIVING THESE PROMISES FOR US PERSONALLY

Read John 15:7–8:

7 If you abide in me, and my words abide in you, ask whatever you wish, and it will be done for you. 8 By this my Father is glorified, that you bear much fruit and so prove to be my disciples.

You abide in Him. That's the relationship. Connected to Him, staying in the Kingdom. Be in Him, walking in Him. Surrendered to Him. Then, as you are doing that, let His Word abide where? In you. We fully understand and have received what He has spoken to us personally. He's spoken to us, and His words to us are in our soul—and now remaining in me at the soul level—what I think, feel, and receive as true. He asks us if we believe it. Then you can pray His will. He said, "If you pray My will, because now you have it, it'll happen." Why will that happen? His will is going to glorify God. What's going to happen? Something unusual. It's not natural. If it's natural, that doesn't glorify anybody, but the flesh. But when it's, "Wow, look at that, this is remarkable," we can give glory to what God just did. Give glory to God automatically because we know and can bear witness that this happened because of Him. He wants us to tell the whole story. We tend to tell just the outcome—God did this thing. Isn't that cool? To give Him the glory, He wants us to tell the whole story. "I asked God what He had to say. He said this. I processed this. I received clarity. I believed it, and it happened." Tell the whole story to encourage people to also have a heart to move into this same place and learn to abide, to hear, to process, and to experience God's magnificent will for them.

Read Mark 11:20–25:

The Lesson from the Withered Fig Tree

[20] As they passed by in the morning, they saw the fig tree withered away to its roots. [21] And Peter remembered and said to him, "Rabbi, look! The fig tree that you cursed has withered." [22] And Jesus answered them, "Have faith in God. [23] Truly, I say to you, whoever says to this mountain, 'Be taken up and thrown into the sea,' and does not doubt in his heart, but believes that what he says will come to pass, it will be done for him. [24] Therefore I tell you, whatever you ask in prayer, believe that you have received[a] it, and it will be yours. [25] And whenever you stand praying, forgive, if you have anything against anyone, so that your Father also who is in heaven may forgive you your trespasses."[b]

____

____

____

____

____

The context here is this: Jesus, on Palm Sunday, is walking into Jerusalem and He passes this fig tree and says, I curse you. He just spoke it and then moved on. He and the disciples are going back out the second day to Bethany to see Mary, Martha, and Lazarus. This illustrates an important element of how Jesus operates with us. He didn't walk Himself over to the tree and say, "I have this big lesson to give you." No, He is just walking past it. What is He looking for? Anybody notice anything? And Peter says, "Hey, that fig tree that you cursed is all withered up. My goodness, look at that." And He just said, "I'm glad you noticed that. Now let Me explain something to you." He says, "Have faith in God." English doesn't interpret this correctly. The Greek says, "Have the faith OF God."

We know something about that. How do you receive the faith of God? He speaks something, authors it, and He finishes it. So, it always is initiated by what He speaks. And Jesus spoke to that tree. That's how it happened. "I spoke to the tree, have the faith of God." And then He says: "Say to the mountain, be cast into the sea." What is that about?

Anything is possible. Everything is possible. Nothing is too difficult for Him, no matter how big and impossible it looks to you. We, in the natural, think that mountains don't move. He said, "You can speak to it and move it, which is necessary to the process of receiving and possessing the promise." You speak to it. Speak what? God's Word? God said, "I'm speaking that." Your participation is critical if you can speak it, where is it? It's in you. You have confidence. You have faith. You have certainty. When do you speak it? Before it happens, which is an important piece of the process. We tend to not want to say this publicly. Why not? If it doesn't happen, I will look like an idiot. It's safer for me to wait until it happens. God says it is necessary for you to have clarity about His will and then believe it. If you do you, then speak it ahead of time publicly. This implies that if you are struggling, you should continue to process until you have clarity (this is why we need each other to assist in this process) and then remain in the Word until you believe it. Faith comes from hearing, and hearing from the Word.

Let's go back to the word "I." Stay with it, until "I am certain that I can speak it. When I speak it ahead of time, it will happen as I spoke it. I join Him in what He already sees—it has happened already." He sees the end; he sees that it already happened. He's not confined to time, which is future. And that's when it's going to happen. He already sees it done. He says: "Join Me in that same spot. You see what I see, it's done. Why? Because I said it. And when you do that and you speak to it and you walk with Me into it, it's going to happen in your timeline in the future. But you have to believe that it is."

In verse 25, He says, "If you have unforgiveness in your heart, you stop the whole process. You're not going anywhere until you receive and live in forgiveness. Let Me forgive you." And if you do, He will remind you that you have unforgiveness in your heart toward someone. We're going to stop. We're not working on the promise anymore. We're working on your heart. And unless you get your heart resolved, you've stopped everything. This is really critical. Why? That's the whole foundation of what we have received from Him and are demonstrating that He is living in us and through us through forgiveness. The promise occurs in the Kingdom. To demonstrate that you're in the Kingdom, you must have forgiveness in your heart, which is His nature. He says, "Your freedom depends on living out My nature." And He is not speaking about reconciliation, which is a different process than forgiveness. Forgiveness is between you and God, which demonstrates that you have His nature within you. Reconciliation is between two parties, so may or may not happen, which is why this is not the condition to receive, believe, and speak the promise to see it happen. This expresses the power of forgiveness as an important indicator of you being in His Kingdom, where His will is fulfilled, and why it is necessary for you to be living there. If you are, you will not be in unforgiveness but in forgiveness, which is a right heart between you and God.

> **Read Matthew 18:18–20:**
>
> [18] Truly, I say to you, whatever you bind on earth shall be bound in heaven, and whatever you loose on earth shall be loosed[a] in heaven. [19] Again I say to you, if two of you agree on earth about anything they ask, it will be done for them by my Father in heaven. [20] For where two or three are gathered in my name, there am I among them."

____

____

____

____

____

We learned that if you pray according to His will, it's going to happen. His words are true and apply to you. It's going to happen. You speak to it based upon your confidence that it's applying to you. It's going to happen. He gives a beautiful way to receive confirmation of His will, upon which the fulfillment of His promise is based. He tells us to go to unity with another believer in whom is also the Holy Spirit, who can confirm His will and what He has spoken. First, you gather in His name. Start the process when you have a problem, when you have something in your life that you need some assistance on, you need a decision to be made, or you have something that's concerning you. Gather in His name by asking what the Father has to say about this as we together seek His will, not your own. We place ourselves, along with two or more others, to have a heart to receive His will. Then, we are to go to unity to receive confirmation, agreement that we together have heard, understood, and have confirmation of His will. Confirmation is in the Spirit, not in negotiation. We do not negotiate what seems to make sense to us. Rather confirmation is with the Spirit, so we know that we know His will, which is best and none better. We stay with it until that specific promise that applies to you becomes clear. Your time is really going to be spent seeking His will, getting clarity about His will—because that's where the promise is fulfilled. You're in unity with what God's will is, and He said, "When you're there, My will is going to be fulfilled; it will be done." And you have the power to bind Satan off from that promise and loose the very power of heaven to fulfill the promise, bringing the supernatural into your circumstance based upon God's will, who has the power to deliver supernaturally His promise and His will for you. This may also include instruction for us to get to the right place for Him to fulfill it. If we have clarity, we then can be obedient to the instruction, as we willingly follow, knowing we are being led to the fulfillment of the promise. This also may involve going to unity to gain clarity.

As we finish this course, we encourage all of you to go back to the truths and the process given us to hear, process, receive, believe, and then speak His promises to us, knowing that we then will experience the promises, possess the promises, and enjoy the wonder and magnificence of the promises for us. We work at it together until there's unity and clarity, and we get to where David went to: God is all powerful and can do it. We know that His words, His promises are true, and this applies to each of us personally in this situation. And then we speak it, and we say, "May it be so. Amen."

Now go through, one at a time, each of your difficult circumstances, issues, questions, decisions, etc. and apply the process to each:

1. **What does the Father have to speak about this—His promise?**

2. **Go to unity and confirm you understand it with clarity.**

3. **How then are you to walk into it and receive His faith—walk with Him and stay with it until you receive the faith.**

4. **Speak it publicly—with confidence.**

5. **Expect to experience it and then give Him the glory!**

____

____

____

____

____

____

____

____

____

www.ingramcontent.com/pod-product-compliance
Lightning Source LLC
Chambersburg PA
CBHW042043110726
48006CB00002B/275